THE
*Archive Photographs*
SERIES

# PERCIVALS
## AIRCRAFT

The most famous Gull of all, the Gull Six flown by Jean Batten on her long-distance flights to Brazil in 1935, to New Zealand in 1936, and from Australia to England in 1937. Impressed into the Royal Air Force in 1940, it survived the war and was purchased back and restored, as shown here, by Percival Aircraft Ltd in January 1946. It was donated to the Shuttleworth Trust in 1961 and maintained by them in an airworthy condition as the last flying example of a Gull Six. However, in February 1995, it was sold to New Zealand's Auckland Airport for static display only. The reported cost was £80,000, whereas the original cost to Jean in 1935 was £1,725. (PAC)

Front Cover Illustration. A line of Proctor 4 and Proctor 3 aircraft awaiting delivery after repair and servicing by the Proctor Repair Unit at Luton. Just visible at top left is one of the last Mosquito aircraft assembled by Percivals at Luton. (RAF Museum No. P100508)

THE
*Archive Photographs*
SERIES

# PERCIVALS
## AIRCRAFT

*Compiled by*
Norman H. Ellison

CHALFORD

First published 1997
Copyright © Norman H. Ellison, 1997

The Chalford Publishing Company
St Mary's Mill, Chalford,
Stroud, Gloucestershire, GL6 8NX

ISBN 0 7524 0774 0

Typesetting and origination by
The Chalford Publishing Company
Printed in Great Britain by
Redwood Books, Trowbridge

*Published to mark the 100th Anniversary*
*of the birth of*
*Edgar Wickner Percival.*

# Contents

The final aircraft of the classic Gull series. The only Procter 6, CF-EHF, originally supplied to Canada as a floatplane, was still flying in 1960 at Oshawa, Ontario. (Photographed by Nick Wolochatiuk on 19 June 1960)

# Introduction

In one of the earlier books* in the *Archive Photographs Series*, author Derek N. James refers to 'the well known names of Britain's pioneering aircraft designers and pilots who founded their own companies. Among them were Sopwith, Handley Page, the Short brothers, Fairey and Blackburn.' All these men founded great companies that designed and built great aeroplanes. There were other great aeronautical engineers who were also pilots and who founded their own companies. Their names became famous all round the world, but their aircraft and their companies were on a much smaller scale than the original great British pioneers.

The British light aircraft industry, now often referred to as general aviation, was dominated by two great pilot engineers during the period 1930 to 1950. Edgar Wickner Percival was born on 23 February 1897 at Albury in New South Wales, Australia. He spent most of his childhood on various farms around Richmond and Sydney. In 1915 he joined an Australian Light Horse regiment and initially saw service in the Middle East but soon transferred to the Royal Flying Corps where, after initial training, he flew solo after twenty-three minutes of tuition. After further training in England he was returned to the Middle East, where he joined No.111 Squadron with which he stayed until the end of the war.

Upon demobilisation in Egypt, he purchased two surplus Avro 504s and a D.H. 6 and had them shipped to Australia. Percival set up a company for commercial aviation, joyriding, charters, aerial surveying and advertising. He also used one of the Avros for racing, finishing fourth in the 1924 Australian Derby. An Avro Avian was added to his fleet in 1927 and he was also involved in aircraft design work. Engaged in this latter activity he came to England and, in July 1928, flew his own Avro Avian in the King's Cup race at Brooklands. He followed this, in September 1928, by flying into second place in the French Light Aeroplane trials at Orly, Paris.

At about this time he was approved by the Air Ministry as a test pilot for seaplanes, landplanes and flying boats. This enabled him to do freelance flying and, during this work he met the aircraft designer Basil B. Henderson. 'Hendy' Henderson had designed and built at Shoreham a single seat ultra light aircraft, the Hendy 281 Hobo. This received its first flight during October 1929, and Percival was the test pilot. Very shortly afterwards Henderson started the design of a two seat version of the Hobo, to be known as the Hendy 302. Built by George Parnall and Co. at Yate, Bristol, Captain Percival flew it in the King's Cup air race in June 1930, at an average speed of 121.51 mph. For a new aeroplane this was indeed an achievement and the next year, in 1931, Percival achieved 145 mph in the Heston to Newcastle race.

In 1931 Henderson started to design a three seat version of the 302, generally known as the Hendy 311. During this time, Capt Percival was working with Saunders-Roe Ltd to design and build the three engined A.24 Mailplane. Following reorganisation of the Saunders-Roe and Spartan companies on the Isle of Wight, Percival sold his interest in the Mailplane and concentrated his efforts on a new aircraft which he called the Gull. Percival had realised the potential of the Hendy 302 aircraft and, with the assistance of R.H. Bound, they designed and built the Gull at the British Aircraft Co. in Maidstone, Kent. This early association with a company with the initials BAC was somewhat prophetic, as it was into another BAC that the Percival Company eventually disappeared.

Whether the Hendy 311 and Percival's Gull were in fact the same design has been debated for many years now, and space does not permit further discussion here. However, the first Gull was officially certified as 'an aircraft of type subsequent to the Hendy 302.' (For further details of the 302/Gull theories see the June and July 1994 issues of *Aeroplane Monthly*). Percival's Gull used the same general design layout as the original Hendy 302, including the patented wing construction invented by Basil Henderson whereby the wing was made to fold about the rear spar. The engine was an inverted Cirrus Hermes and this immensely improved its speed. It also established the classic Gull appearance. The aircraft was built very quickly as, after test flying, Capt Percival flew it around Britain in the 1932 King's Cup air race during 8/9 July 1932, at an average speed of 142.73 mph.

* *The Gloster Aircraft Company* compiled by Derek N. James from Chalford Publishing.

Note. The information included in brackets at the end of a caption represents the source of the photograph.

The prototype Gull G-ABUR on an early test flight. Clearly shown is the original Henderson-type fin and rudder. (PAC)

Alterations to the fin, rudder shape and a navigation light result in the standard Gull profile, with the original strut-type wheel units. (PAC PY1600)

Christmas 1933.

————

Wishing you a Happy Christmas
and New Year.

from

*Mr. & Mrs. R. H. Bound.*

A Christmas card sent by R.H. Bound to the employees of the Lowe-Wylde British Aircraft Company at Maidstone, Kent, where G-ABUR was built.

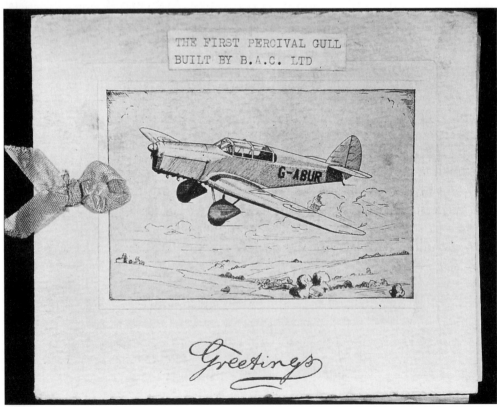

THE FIRST PERCIVAL GULL
BUILT BY B.A.C. LTD

The front of the same Christmas card. Note the later revised cabin roof structure in this pen and ink drawing.

# One

# The Classic Gulls

At the height of the economic depression that hit the world in the early 1930s, what separated Percival from most other aeronautical designers of the period was the fact that he managed to acquire the financial resources to think seriously about quantity production. His dynamic personality, together with his prestige as an air racing pilot, probably helped him set up a company and obtain the necessary finance during a period of insecurity after the Great Depression of 1930. In this he was assisted by Lt Cdr E.B.W. Leake, and the Percival Aircraft Company was officially formed in 1933. Capt Percival was appointed the managing director and chief designer. The head office was established at 20 Grosvenor Square, London, and included a drawing office with R.H. Bound as chief draughtsman. George Parnall and Company then received a contract to build twenty-four Gull Four aircraft which were completed during 1933 and 1934. Thus the Gull was the first low-wing monoplane to be put into production in England, and the selling price was £1,250.

Sales of the Gull were brisk and helped by a record flight to Australia by Sir Charles Kingsford Smith. He had arranged to become Percival's agent in Australia and flew the first one home in a record time of 7 days, 4 hours and 44 minutes during October 1933.

A small factory had also been set up at Gravesend Airport in Kent early in 1934 and here, Percival and Bound designed and built the initial small Mew Gull single-seat racing aircraft. This had its first flight in March 1934 and, after being certified, Capt Percival flew it in the King's Cup air race on 13 July 1934. After the initial Parnall batch of Gulls were built, Percival then set up its own production line at Gravesend. At about the same time, Arthur A. Bage joined the company as chief draughtsman and all the later Gulls, the first batch of Vega Gulls and the initial revised version of the Mew Gulls, were built here. W.A. Summers also joined the company as works manager and Jack Lavender was the licensed ground engineer. The company remained at Gravesend until the final move was made to Luton, Bedfordshire, at the end of 1936.

During this period, Capt Percival was, in effect, the company's test pilot and publicity department. In this latter occupation he flew in the UK air races each year. Although always amongst the leaders in the premier race, the King's Cup race, he often flew the fastest speed but never actually won the race; the handicappers were usually blamed for this contempt of the captain's piloting skills. He also flew many long-distance flights to Europe and Africa. However, most publicity came from the other long-distance record flyers of the 1930s, namely Jean Batten, C.J. Melrose, Amy Johnson, H.L. Brook, Charles W.A. Scott, Beryl Markham, Jimmy Broadbent and Alex Henshaw as well as Charles Gardner and Giles Guthrie, Edgar Percival's annual rivals in the King's Cup race who also flew in Mew Gulls. All these flights were fully detailed in the aviation periodicals, the daily popular newspapers, the radio and the cinema newsreels. Consequently the Gulls did not need much advertising and probably almost sold themselves. Percival's company advertising was often an individual tribute to the latest record that had been established.

Probably the greatest triumph of Percival-built aircraft as a group, was during the 1936 England to South Africa Schlesinger Race. Of the original fourteen entrants, seven were built by Percivals. On the 29 September, only nine aircraft started the race from Portsmouth Airport and only one arrived at Johannesburg on 1 October – the Vega Gull flown by Charles W.A. Scott and Giles Guthrie. Their time was 52 hours, 56 minutes and 48.2 seconds, but many of the other aircraft flew far into Africa.

Amid all the resultant publicity, to ease its production capacity problems Percival Aircraft Ltd moved to a new factory at the recently established Luton Corporation Airport. Production of Vega Gulls was the main activity. Twenty-two Vegas had been built at Gravesend and a further seventy-seven were built at Luton, the last one being delivered on 27 July 1939. The other activity after the move to Luton was the design and production of the twin-engined Q-6 aircraft. The prototype had its first flight at Luton on the 14 September 1937, by Capt Percival, and twenty-seven were produced before the Second World War brought production to an end. Of this total, eight were built under an Air Ministry contract and were known as Petrels. Most of the civilian Q-6 aircraft were absorbed into the RAF at the outbreak of the war and these were also given the name Petrel.

The 1939 King's Cup air race, which was scheduled to take place at Birmingham Airport on Saturday 2 September, could have been Capt Percival's year to win. He was the strongest competitor and aircraft entrant, although a new handicap system might have been his downfall. However, the race was cancelled ahead of the outbreak of the Second World War the following day.

Gull Four G-ACFY, sold to the A.V. Roe and Co. Ltd, Woodford, in 1935, showing the revised clear cabin roof. (PAC PY1598)

Gull Four G-ACHM owned by Brian Allen Aviation Ltd, Croydon. The nose-up attitude of the early Gull is quite distinct. La Palace is presumed to be in France, as G-ACHM was sold there in May 1936. (PAC)

Gull Four G-ACJV at Yate, Bristol. It was sold to Sir Charles Kingsford Smith in October 1933, who flew it to Australia in a new record time of 7 days, 4 hours and 44 minutes. The large 60 gallon long-range fuel tank is mounted in the rear of the cockpit. (Fairfax Photo Library, Sydney)

Gull Four G-ACPA with revised cockpit entry door. (PAC PY1601B)

Gull Six G-ADEP, the company demonstrator aircraft, used by Capt Percival for his day flight to Oran and back. Note the final version of the doors and the wheel fairings that were used for the rest of the Gull and Vega Gull aircraft. (PAC PY673)

Gull Six G-ADKX in its two tone yellow and red colour scheme of the Shell Petroleum Company. It was based in Cairo, Egypt, until impressed into the RAF in Egypt in November 1940. (PAC)

Gull Six ZK-AES and its owner Lt P. Randolph. The aircraft was flown out to New Zealand during October and November 1936. (PAC)

Gull Six G-ADPR was sold to Jean Batten on 15 September 1935 for £1,725, her twenty-sixth birthday, and used for her last three long-distance flights from 1935 to 1937. It survived the war in RAF service. (Photographed by Norman H. Ellison at Luton Airport, 16 August 1949)

Captain Edgar Percival in front of the original Mew Gull. (PAC)

The first Mew Gull G-ACND in March 1934, with a Napier Javelin engine. Flown by Percival in the 1934 King's Cup air race on 13 July, it crashed in France during the Coupe Michelin race in October 1934. (PAC)

The second G-ACND revised Mew Gull with a Gipsy Six engine. It was flown by Capt Percival in the 1935 race season, including the King's Cup race in which it was placed sixth at an average speed of 208.9 mph.

For the 1936 UK to South Africa Schlesinger Race, Percivals Aircraft built three more Mew Gulls. Here Capt Percival tests the second one, ZS-AHN, which was built for Capt S.S. Halse of South Africa. It was forced out of the race at Belgrade due to bad fuel and later sold to Alex Henshaw as G-AEXF. (PAC)

Captain Percival taxis out in his final Mew Gull G-AFAA for another race. It had shorter wings and a 205 hp D.H. Gipsy Six Series 2 engine. He finished third in the 1937 race, at a speed of 238.7 mph.

Mew Gull 2A G-AFAA at the official opening of Luton Airport on 16 July 1938. (Luton Museum Service)

Mew Gull G-AFAA on 7 July 1945, painted up to represent a crashed German aircraft, in a comic fire brigade display at the annual Percivals' employees' Field Day. The Mew Gull had been damaged during the war and was burnt later in the afternoon, a tragic and unnecessary destruction of a famous piece of British aviation history. This is the only known photograph of this event and it had to be copied direct from an old copy of a South Bedfordshire newspaper, remaining in the vaults of the Luton Library.

The Mew Gull G-AEXF. The lower revised canopy was introduced in 1938 and helped Alex Henshaw win the King's Cup air race; he then made his record flight to Cape Town and return in February 1939. (Norman H. Ellison)

The Mew Gull G-AEXF at the rained-out 1951 King's Cup air race at Hatfield. It had been in store in France during the war. (Norman H. Ellison)

The Mew Gull G-AEXF again, at Luton Airport. The canopy had been raised again to suit a larger pilot. In this form Peter Clifford won the 1955 King's Cup air race at 213 mph. It is now kept at Old Warden with the Shuttleworth Trust. (PAC PY4211)

The instrument panel and cockpit of G-AEXF in 1955. (PAC PY4212)

Eaton Green Farm, consisting of 308 acres, was purchased in 1936 by Luton Borough Council at a cost of £100 an acre, for the future Luton Airport. The farmhouse is just off the right side of the picture; the Percival Aircraft Co. leased 10 acres to build a factory over the chalk tracts. (*The Luton News*; Luton Museum Service)

The new Percivals' factory in the course of construction. (PAC)

The P.7 open cockpit Touring Gull built in 1935 for the Maharajah of Jodphur. There are only two known photographs of this special aircraft. (PAC)

The other photograph of the P.7 Gull. Later registered in India as VT-AGV, it obviously did not last very long, as the crashed remains were returned to Luton in 1938. (PAC)

Mr Arthur A. Bage, chief engineer up to 1948. (PAC)

Vega Gull Series 2, G-AEYC, was the company demonstrator up to 1939. After wartime service it was used by various operators until 1960 – one of the last Gulls to survive. At the nose stands John Silvester, who started with the company in 1937 and, now retired, still lives in Luton. (PAC)

Mr Jack Lavender, service manager. (PAC)

Vega Gull VP-KCC, being pushed out of the hangar at Gravesend, for delivery to Beryl Markham. Jack Lavender is at the wing root. (The estate of Beryl Markham)

Vega Gull VP-KCC on its nose in the bog at Ballerne Cove, Nova Scotia on 5 September 1936, after Beryl's trans-Atlantic flight. (The estate of Beryl Markham)

Luton Airport and the Percivals Aircraft factory in 1937. The large hangars proudly announce 'Luton Corporation' in large black letters, and the old farmhouse is the only original farm building left standing. The view is to the northwest and shows Round Green, Stopsley and the Warden Hills. (Luton Museum Service)

The first Vega Gull for the Secretary of State for Air; L7272 was later used by the air attaché to the British Embassy in Buenos Aires as G-AFWG. (PAC)

A P.10C Vega Gull, when the last cockpit windscreen shape was almost a Proctor. This Vega Gull P5993 did not survive the war. (PAC)

Vega Gull G-AFEA, the Vega Gull used by Alex Henshaw and his father for a survey flight around Africa in 1938 when planning his record flight in the Mew Gull in 1939. Note the family Jaguar parked alongside. (Alex Henshaw)

The Vega Gull G-AFEA, post-war at Croydon, after wartime service with Gloster Aircraft Ltd. It was now painted a creamy-white all over, with dark green letters. This was as it was known to the author when it was based at Luton in 1948. (Mike Eacock)

Vega Gull G-AFBC, which was sold to A.R. Coleman, Norwich, in 1937. It survived the war and had several owners until it crashed at Eastleigh in July 1954. (PAC)

Vega Gull G-AFIE. This was sold to Smith's Aircraft Instruments Ltd, at Hatfield, and used by them until it was destroyed when Hendon Airfield was bombed on the night of 7 October 1940. (PAC)

Vega Gull VH-ABS was used by the Shell Asiatic Petroleum Company in Australia, and had a yellow and red colour scheme similar to that of Gull Six G-ADKX (see page 15). It was flown all round Australia on sales tours. (Reproduced from *Winged Shell* by Hugh Scanlan, by permission of the publisher, Alison Hodge, 1987)

A model of a proposed two seat training aircraft designed to Air Ministry Specification T.1/37. Four other companies also tendered to this specification: Heston, Airspeed (AS.36), Parnall (Type 382) and Miles (M.15). Only the Parnall and Miles designs were built, but neither were selected for production contracts. (PAC)

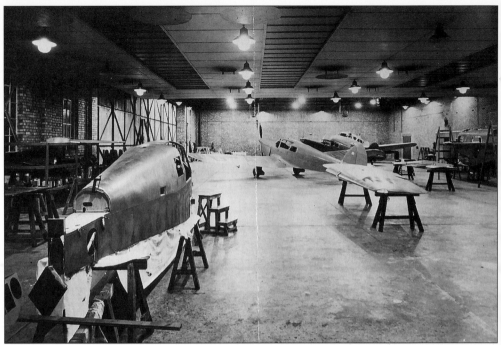

The fabric and spray shop at Luton. The Vega Gull in the centre is G-AFAU which became the company demonstration aircraft. It survived the war in the RAF to become G-AIIT with St Christopher Travel-Ways Ltd, but its luck ran out at Croydon in November 1947 when it was scrapped. (PAC)

The first of two Q.6 aircraft suppled to Lithuania in 1938. They both survived the initial Russian invasion and were used on the Riga to Velikie and Luki to Moscow routes. However, both were destroyed during the later German invasion. (PAC)

A line-up of four Q.6 aircraft. YI-ROH was delivered to King Ghazi of Iraq, and then into the RAF Middle East in 1941. It was lost during service with the Iraq Communications Flight during February 1943. (PAC)

One of the Q.6 aircraft built with a retractable undercarriage. This one was VH-ABY and was sold to the Australian Air Board. (PAC copy)

Two Q.6 aircraft were supplied to the Egyptian Air Force. (PAC)

The last six Q.6 aircraft built at Luton were supplied to the Royal Air Force and named Petrel for communications duties. (PAC)

# Two
# Second World War Activities

In 1938, during the build-up of the Royal Air Force before the outbreak of war, Percivals received a small contract to supply some Q-6 and Vega Gulls to the Air Ministry to be used for communications and also abroad, in several countries where an air attaché was attached to a British Embassy. Later it was realised that there was a great need for training aircraft for navigators and wireless operators so in February 1939, Percivals began incorporating the necessary design requirements into the Vega Gull design. The name Proctor was chosen in place of Vega Gull, and they were built in three versions: the Proctor 1 for communications duties and the Proctor 2 and 3 for wireless operator training. The prototype Proctor was flown at Luton by David Bay on 8 October 1939 and 247 were subsequently delivered to the RAF and the Royal Navy. These were followed by 200 Proctor 2s and 438 Proctor 3s, most of which were built by sub-contractors. They were used at all the signal schools in the UK and also in Australia, South Africa, India, Ceylon and Trinidad. The Royal Navy versions had a quick release dinghy, with automatic inflation gear, in the wing centre section.

The ultimate Proctor version was the larger Mark 4. This was a complete re-design of the basic Proctor airframe and the first flight of the prototype took place on 16 March 1942. The new design enabled the aircraft to be quickly converted from one training duty to another; 258 of these were built, mostly by sub-contractor F. Hills and Sons of Manchester because the Luton factory, with its larger capacity, was required to build bigger aircraft.

On 15 March 1940, Percivals received a contract to build Airspeed Oxford twin engined trainers for the RAF. After a reorganisation of the factory, the first Oxford built under this contract was delivered to the RAF on 11 October 1940. Eventually 1,355 Oxfords were built before the factory was converted, once again, to build bombers.

On 3 June 1943 a contract was received for the factory to build de Havilland Mosquito Mark 16 bombers and the first of these was delivered on 5 June 1944, 1 year and 2 days later. During this time the original Percivals' factory had to have many alterations, including the building of new engine test houses. After 195 of the Mark 16 Mosquitoes had been constructed there was another change on the production line, and fifty of the very specialised long-range photographic reconnaissance Mark 34 Mosquitoes were built, intended for use by the RAF South East Asia Command against the Japanese.

During the war the number of employees increased from about 300 in June 1939 to a peak of 1,300 in 1941. At that time most of the work was sub-contracted to small local firms. The factory was bombed twice during 1940, the first time on 27 August and the last time on 24 September. Little damage occurred during the first high-altitude daylight raid but during the second raid, two parachute mines were dropped during the night. The first exploded nearby; the second landed in the middle of the factory but did not explode.

Changes in the company structure and management also occurred at this time. The original Percival Aircraft Company was changed at the end of 1936 into a limited company and a board of directors was introduced. During 1938 the Marquess of Londonderry was elected chairman and, in March 1940, Capt P.D. Acland, who had been the Aviation Manager of Vickers Ltd. just after the First World War, was made managing director. Capt Percival resigned from the company and Arthur Bage became the chief designer.

Percivals' did keep design control of the Proctor during the war, and a Proctor Repair Unit was set up in the small centre hangar on the airfield. This unit repaired and serviced some 847 Proctor aircraft and also carried out some specialised conversions. One of these, in 1944, was a special Proctor 4 for the use of the Duke of Gloucester in Australia.

The prototype Proctor 1, P5998, outside the experimental hangar, having its engine checked before its first flight on 8 October 1939. (PAC PY1537)

An early production Proctor 1 at Luton. (PAC)

The second prototype of the Proctor 4, LA589, with the restricted photography 'P' ahead of the national markings. It has all the radio equipment fitted and is, therefore, the training version for the RAF. (RAF Museum P100505)

The prototype Proctor 4 aircraft, LA586, had its first flight from Luton on 16 March 1942. This was the four seat communications version. (RAF Museum P100509)

de Havilland Mosquito assembly at Percivals. PF634, in the centre, was one of the special P.R. Mark 34A versions intended for Far East service. The RR Merlin 114A engine assemblies can be see ready for installation as a complete unit. (PAC)

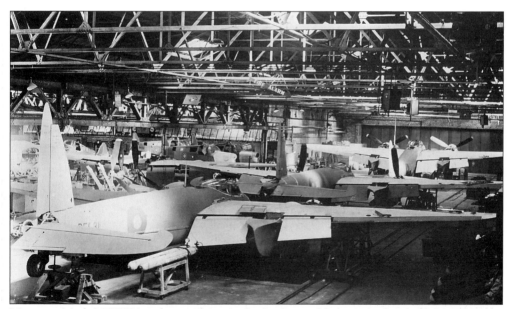

Mosquito Mark 34 PF631 and two others on the final assembly line. At the rear left can be seen the first four Proctor 5s being converted from Mark 4 aircraft. This photo must therefore have been taken between June and November 1945. (PAC)

The repair and service department at Luton Airport with various Proctor 3 and 4 aircraft receiving attention. Behind the front Mark 3 is another Mark 3, DX243, with a Mark 4 on the left. The service hangar was the small centre hangar next to the large hangar at the end with 'Luton Corporation' painted on it. (PAC)

A line-up of Proctor aircraft ready for delivery from the Repair Unit, including P229, (Mark 4) LZ572, (Mark 3) and Z7189, a Mark 2. This is not the same line of aircraft as on the cover. (PAC, probably from the original by Charles E. Brown.)

This Manchester-built Proctor 3, DX238, came up for sale from the RAF after the war and was allocated G-ALUK, but was broken up for spares at Croft. (PAC)

Proctor 4, NP389, after repair at the Service Unit, with various patches of red dope still visible on the wing-root fairing and the fin. (PAC)

Proctor 3, W-1, a post-war export to the Dutch Air Force. (PAC)

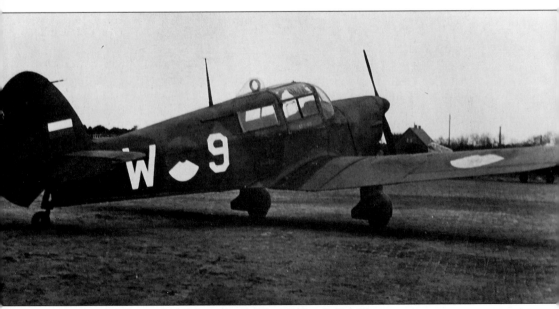

Proctor 4, W-9, transferred from the RAF to Holland. (PAC)

44

# Three
# A Takeover

Once the end of the war was in sight, aircraft companies began to make plans for post-war activities. Other companies also joined in what was expected to be a time of great prosperity now that the world had made great advances in aircraft and air travel. Consequently, Percivals Aircraft was bought out by the shipping and oil company, Hunting and Son Ltd, of Newcastle-on-Tyne in September 1944. Capt Acland retired at the end of 1944 and in 1945, the board of directors of Percivals' comprised Mr P.L. Hunting (chairman), Mr W.A. Summers (managing director), with other directors L. Hunting, C.P.M. Hunting, B.N. Whiteside, K.D. Morgan and M.R. Cook; J.A. Mackenzie was appointed general manager. There was no change in the company name.

Production of the Mosquito aircraft continued until the end of the war, but plans were made to produce a replacement for the pre-war Vega Gulls. Starting as a basis with the design of the special conversion that had been produced for the Duke of Gloucester, the result was the Proctor 5 aircraft. This was put into production soon after the war ended as a full four seat private and touring aircraft costing £2,900.

A batch of 150 Proctor 5 aircraft was built, with sales all round the world. Once again the initial aircraft sold themselves, helped by several long-distance flights, just as the Vega Gulls were sold before the war. Two delivery flights were made by Jim Mollison and flights to Australia were made by Nevil Shute Norway, A.J. Bradshaw and wartime pilots flying home their own Proctors. However, when the RAF began releasing its surplus wartime Proctors, sales of the new aircraft almost stopped. As the Luton factory had received a large order for the new three-seat Prentice training aircraft in December 1945, many Proctor 5 aircraft had to be stored to provide factory space.

The Prentice trainer was Percivals first all-metal aircraft. The first prototype flew on 30 March 1946 and eventually 523 were built at Luton and at Brough, Yorkshire, at the works of the Blackburn and General Aircraft Ltd. Included in this total were Prentices built for export to India, Lebanon and Argentina. At least forty-two were also built in India by Hindustan Industries.

Simultaneously, Percivals were also building a light twin-engined aircraft, the Prince, which was built in considerable numbers for the next ten years. The first Prince flew at Luton on 13 May 1948 and developed versions were known as the Prince 3 and Survey Prince. The RAF and other air forces placed large orders for the Pembroke version, with longer wings and service equipment, the civilian version of which was called the President. At the end of 1948 Arthur Bage retired as chief designer and his replacement, L.G. Frise, was appointed to the position of chief engineer.

Percivals' final piston engined aircraft was the two-seat Provost training aircraft. This started its design life as a two-seat aircraft with a DH Gypsy Queen engine, and was offered to the Air Ministry as the aircraft that the company thought the Prentice should have been. Two prototypes with a Cheetah engine were ordered, and the first one had its initial flight on 23 February 1950. After competitive trials against another Provost with an Alvis Leonides engine as well as aircraft from another company, the Air Ministry agreed, and the Provost entered quantity production but with an Alvis engine. The Prentice had a very short service life and a large number were disposed of to the civil market but, for many reasons, Prentices were often later to be seen on heaps of scrap metal.

The initial deliveries of Provosts were made to the Royal Air Force in 1953 and the last one remained in service until 1969. They were exported to many countries including Rhodesia, Ireland, Sudan, Muscat and Oman, Iraq, Burma and Malaya.

The Proctor 5, G-AGTC, was the company demonstrator aircraft for many years until replaced by G-AKYA. TC was later was used for general duties until it was damaged beyond repair at Malaga, Spain, on 2 May 1969. Its twenty-three years of service made it one of the longest surviving Proctor 5 aircraft. (PAC)

Jim Mollison delivered Proctor 5, G-AGTA, to Rio de Janeiro, Brazil, by air, 28 January 1946 to 3 February 1946. The aircraft had a 45 gallon drop tank under the fuselage in addition to a 55 gallon long-range fuel tank in the cockpit. However, G-AGTA did not last long in Brazil as it was dismantled in December 1947. (PAC copy)

One of two Proctor 5 aircraft delivered to Percivals' Aircraft's sister company Hunting Air Travel at Luton Airport. Note the Mosquito just visible to the right; this photograph must have been taken in late 1945. (Mike Eacock)

The Proctor 5, G-AHGN, purchased by the Ministry of Civil Aviation for the use of the British Civil Air Attaché in America. It is flying over the Capital Building, Washington DC, probably piloted by Sir Peter Masefield. (PAC; original source unknown)

The standard Percivals method of transporting export aircraft. The square-nose army-surplus Bedford truck is taking Proctor 5, CC-PEB, to the packing depot in London. (PAC)

A Proctor 5 and the Percivals' factory during the filming of the novel *Mr Denning Drives North* on 6 May 1951. Many employees were used as extras, including crowd shots, scenes inside the factory and cameo appearances by well known members of the management. (Luton Museum Service)

The well-known author Mr Nevil Shute Norway and his wife taking delivery of his Proctor 5 aircraft, G-AKIW, in April 1948. They later flew it to Australia in 1949, where he registered it as VH-DIW. (Mike Keep collection)

The delivery ceremony. Left to right: -?-, Mrs Norway, one of the Hunting family, Nevil Shute Norway, David Bay (sales manager), -?-, Jack Lavender (service manager). (Mike Keep collection)

Proctor 5 aircraft, VN 896, on the scales inside the final assembly hangar among the second batch of Prince aircraft. (Photographed by Norman Ellison in January 1953)

A line-up of Proctor 5 aircraft awaiting delivery in June 1948 to the Arab Airways Association, Amman, Jordan. They were all later used by the Arab Legion Air Force. Note the building on the horizon. This was the Luton Isolation Hospital and it had its own entrance road to the west. This road is now the wide, main entrance road to Luton International Airport. (PAC PY914)

Another Proctor 5 exported to Australia in 1946. Note the strong camouflage lines on the doors of the Service department doors. (Mike Eacock)

The first of two Proctor 5 aircraft for the Lebanese Air Force. There are three apprentices aboard for the very popular photographic ride. (PAC)

Two Proctor 5 aircraft awaiting delivery to the Syrian Air Force. (PAC)

The Proctor 5 in which the author had his first ever flight. It was one of the popular apprentice photographic flights on the 17 September 1948. G-AKYA was visiting Sywell PFA Rally when the author visited there in 1960.

The end of the Proctor line in 1948. Here are thirteen Proctor 5 aircraft in storage, awaiting transfer to Percivals' sister company Field Aviation Services Ltd at Croydon. Only about half of them ever gained flight status. (PAC)

A Proctor 4 aircraft, G-AOAR, visiting Rearsby, Leicester, in about 1961 whilst the author worked at Auster Aircraft Ltd. Note the warped state of the fuselage plywood, a common aging effect of early synthetic-type glues on plywood. (Norman H. Ellison)

One of the few post-war record attempts using a Percivals aircraft was by Mrs Richarda Morrow-Tait, with navigator Michael Townsend, ex-RAF undergraduate, who planned a flight at the end of 1948 in a Proctor 4 aircraft. She hoped to be the first woman to fly around the world from Croydon, via Marseilles, North Africa, Egypt, Saudi Arabia, India, Burma, China, Japan, The Aleutians, Canada, Greenland, Iceland, Scotland and back to Cambridge. Here they are leaving Gravesend. (Associated Press, London)

Leaving Cambridge on 18 August 1948 for Croydon, Morrow-Tait and Townsend planned to be away for six weeks. Note the long-range tank in the cockpit, similar to the tanks used in the pre-war Gulls and Vega Gulls. (Associated Press, London)

The Morrow-Tait Proctor 4, G-AJMU, arriving at Haneda Airforce Base, Japan on 27 October 1948, well behind their initial schedule. (Associated Press, New York)

Mrs Richarda Morrow-Tait stepping out of the Proctor 4 at Haneda Airforce Base. After experiencing engine trouble for several days, they reached Tok, Alaska, on 21 November where, in a temperature of minus 30 degrees (F) the Proctor was wrecked in a landing on the Alaska Highway. (Associated Press, New York)

The one and only Proctor 6 aircraft on a test-flight from Rochester works of Short Brothers and Harland. It was built for the Hudson Bay Trading Company of Toronto, Canada, and was registered CF-EHF upon its arrival there. (PAC)

The trial installation of the floats and their struts to the basic Proctor fuselage. Note the tailwheel is still there. Not yet installed was the special engine, a DH Gipsy Queen 32 of 250 hp. The floats were moved forward before the first flight. (PAC)

Luton Airport just after the war ended in 1945. There are three DH Mosquito aircraft on the ramp and only two Proctors, and the airfield circle and name has been restored. The Spittlesea Isolation Hospital is at the top right. The crease in the photo was in the copied photograph.

The Percival Aircraft Ltd factory on the right, with D. Napier & Son test facility and hangars to the left, behind the original three Luton Corporation hangars at the front. This photograph was probably taken later in 1946 as there are no Mosquitoes on the field, but one of the three DH Tiger Moths is still in wartime civil markings. Also evident are two civil DH Dragon Rapides, two Proctors in military markings and three Proctors in civil markings; the Proctor 5 in the centre is registered G-AGTF. A Hawker Tempest stands outside the Napier hangars. (Luton Museum Service)

The first post-war extension was the machine shop (lower floor), whilst the upper floor to the left was for structural testing, and to the right was the lofting floor. Below this were the photographic shop and darkrooms necessary to handle the reproductions from the master loft plates of the lofting template for factory use. (PAC)

The extension to the main office block being built in about 1950. The original part to the right included the planning and tool design offices. The new buildings later accommodated the management, sales, stress and aircraft design departments. The road was the main entry road up to the old farmhouse. (PAC)

The prototype Prentice trainer TV163 in its original form. (Mike Eacock)

A flying view of the Prentice prototype TV163. (PAC)

The engine installation of TV163, a 230 hp de Havilland Gipsy Queen 30-2, with the original exhaust system of six separate stubs. (Mike Eacock)

The second Prentice TV166, painted all-yellow, with fin guard and anti-spin parachute installation. (Mike Keep collection)

The first revision to the fin and rudder shapes to try to improve the dismal spinning characteristics of the Prentice. Here, TV163 has also been fitted with an anti-spin parachute installation. (HPAC PY315)

Another trial installation to solve the spinning problems of the Prentice was to raise the tailplane and elevator up the fin clear of the fuselage. Note the trailing static 'bomb' below the wing and fuselage area. (PAC)

The most drastic revision to the Prentice outline was to introduce twin fins and rudders. This aircraft, VN684, did at least get a final paint scheme. (PAC PY1558)

Also fitted to the twin fins and rudder version of the Prentice were turned-up wing tips. These had the effect of increasing the dihedral of the wings. (PAC)

Prentice VR210 was temporarily registered G-AKLG for an overseas sales tour; here it stands in front of the old farmhouse that became the airport manager's office. (PAC PY692)

During its overseas sales tour the words 'Percival Prentice' on the engine cowling were translated into Arabic and Greek. (PAC PY1014)

The eventual standard shape of the rudder, with anti-spin strakes on the fuselage. Here VR225 is the final production version of the Prentice T. Mk.1. (Mike Eacock)

Production of the Prentice aircraft took place in the new final assembly extension to the main factory. TV177 was one of the pre-production batch being brought up to the final production standard. (PAC)

One of the export aircraft for the Argentine Air Force being test flown from Luton. Aboard are two apprentices enjoying the photographic flight. (PAC)

A trailer, improved from those previously used for Proctor exports, being loaded with this Prentice for export to Argentina. (PAC PY1278)

The final assembly line of Prentices during 1949/50; the author worked at this position for many months during his apprenticeship. Prentices for the RAF as well as Argentina and Lebanon, are in the foreground. (PAC PY1476)

Prentice VR211 at the ARAEE Boscombe Down in 1957. This aircraft was one of the last Prentices in RAF service and the last to be sold off as surplus. It was registered G-ARGA in 1960 but was scrapped at Minworth Metals Ltd, Birmingham, shortly afterwards. (Mike Keep collection)

The Prentice engine did not require many connections when installed into the aircraft. (PAC PY1048)

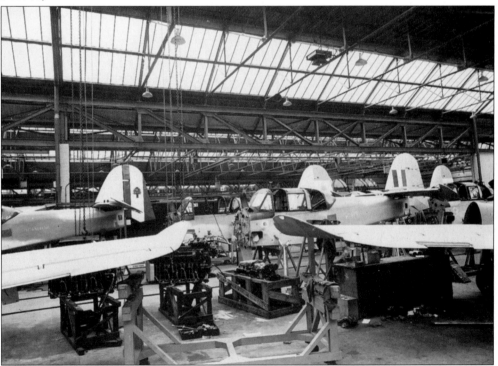

The de Havilland Gipsy Queen 30 engines arrived from de Havilland Engines in simple wooden crates; the equipment around the engine was fitted while it stood on top of the shipping crate. (Mike Keep collection)

The Prentice had a service life in the Royal Air Force of only six years, before replacement started in 1955. Most of them were flown to either Southend or Croydon with temporary civil markings. (Unknown)

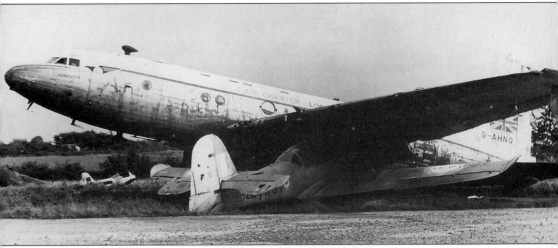

Prentice VS745 resting at Southend, as G-APJF, under the wing of Avro Super Trader 4B G-AHNO, which was scrapped in August 1959 after three years service with Air Charter Ltd. This provides an approximate date for this photograph. (Unknown)

Prentice VR250 after arrival at Stanstead as G-APJA. It was not converted to civil use, and was later broken up along with most of the other 253 Prentices. (Unknown)

The only Prentice Mark 2 and the prototype Prince G-ALCM at the 1948 SBAC display at Farnborough. (PAC PY1126)

The Merganser prototype G-AHMH. As the 296 hp DH Gipsy Queen 51 engines were not put into production, only one Merganser was completed. This had its first flight at Luton on 9 May 1947 but was scrapped just over one year later. (PAC)

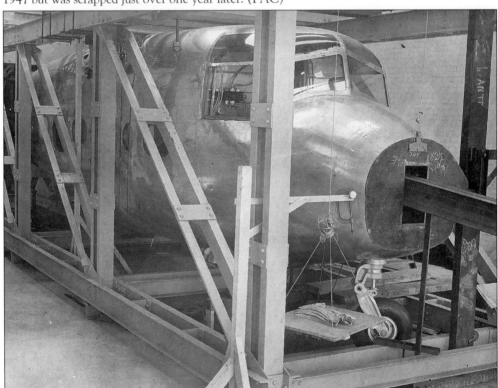

The second Merganser fuselage undergoing structural testing. (PAC)

A Prince G-AMPR awaiting delivery to the Standard Motor Co. Ltd, Coventry. The original wooden control tower is to the right. (Norman H. Ellison, September 1952)

This Prince was sold to South Africa as ZS-DGX, but is here standing in front of the new airport control tower built in 1952. (Norman H. Ellison, September 1952)

One of the early Sea Prince C. Mk.1 aircraft, WF137, was delivered to the Royal Navy for the use of the Flag Officer (Air) Home, as an Admiral's barge. This aircraft is still in existence at Lasham airfield. (PAC PY1928)

The original prototype Prince G-ALCM was used for many experimental installations, including the new nose section for the Sea Prince T. Mk.1 aircraft, and also for a tailplane with dihedral which was found to be unnecessary. G-ALCM was eventually dismantled at Luton in May 1956. (Norman H. Ellison, January 1953)

One of the many Princes sold to the Shell Refining and Marketing Co. Ltd. This one was used in Singapore as VR-SDR, and Borneo as VR-UDR. (PAC)

Another Prince for Shell, VR-SDB, for use in Singapore. On each side are two of the Sea Prince T. Mk. 1 training aircraft for the Royal Navy. The author had seventeen flights, (33 hrs, 15 mins) of observer training in these in 1954. (Norman H. Ellison, January 1953)

Most of the Prince aircraft for Shell were collected and flown away by Group Captain Douglas Bader, the wartime British aviation hero, who founded and became the Managing Director of Shell Aviation Ltd. Here he is ready to fly the first one, G-ALJA, out to Singapore and then on to Borneo. (Reproduced from *Winged Shell* by Hugh Scanlan by permission of the publisher Alison Hodge, 1987)

One of Shell's fleet of Princes, VR-UDC, at Kuching, Sarawak in 1954. The Prince was originally G-AMLY, and then went to Venezuela in 1952. (Reproduced from *Winged Shell* by Hugh Scanlan by permission of the publisher Alison Hodge, 1987)

The longer nose on this Prince is one of the special P.54 Survey Princes that were built. HB-HOF was sold to an aerial survey company in Switzerland. (PAC)

The prototype P.66 Pembroke, WV698, for the Royal Air Force. These aircraft were used for general duties, including an eight seat transporter, freight, or six stretcher air ambulance roles. (Photographed in the unpainted condition by Norman H. Ellison, January1953)

The Pembroke was also sold to other NATO countries, including Belgium and Germany. This one, OT-ZAA, was the first of the batch for Belgium. (PAC)

The new final assembly hangar full of Pembrokes for the RAF and for Belgium. The Provost assembly line is just visible in the old, original assembly line. (PAC)

The first of three President aircraft for an airline in Spain. EC-APA was not delivered and was later used by the British Aircraft Corporation as a communications aircraft between Filton and France during the Concorde years. (PAC)

The third President aircraft for Spain, EC-APC. This aircraft was sold to the Sudanese Air Force in March 1960. (PAC)

A President awaiting delivery to the Danish Air Force in July 1959. Number 697 was later sold off to a Danish company as OY-AVA. (PAC)

One Pembroke aircraft was delivered to the Ministry of Civil Aviation and based at Stansted with the radio and flying unit. G-APMO had one of the longest lives, as it was not withdrawn from use until July 1970. (PAC)

The prototype P.56 Provost trainer, WE 522, with the original Armstrong Siddeley Cheetah engine. Its first flight was on 23 February 1950. (PAC PY1825)

The second P.56 Prototype, WE530, with the Cheetah engine and the revised 'bent down' rear fuselage to lower the tailplane ten inches. (Mike Eacock)

The installation of the 420 hp Armstrong Siddeley Cheetah 18 engine into the Provost prototypes. (PAC PN750)

The trial installation of the 550 hp Alvis Leonides 25 engine into the third Provost prototype WG503. The elephant ears for cooling had yet to be fitted, as the aircraft's first flight had not yet revealed their necessity. (PAC PN1680)

The third prototype Provost, still painted up as the P.56 and the Hunting Horn badge, after sales demonstration flights. (HPAL PY2305)

The Provost production line, where, in years past, Prentices and Mosquitoes had stood in line. (PAC)

A formation take-off of four Provosts at the annual SBAC air display at Farnborough. The year must be about 1953 as they are in-service aircraft. (HPAL)

A shop full of aircraft. Provosts are on the 'old' production line with Sea Prince T.Mk. 1 aircraft in the newer assembly bay in about 1953 or 1954. (PAC PY4183)

An exported Provost, FM1039, for the Malayan Air Force. The presence of a Scottish Aviation Twin-Pioneer aircraft may indicate that this Provost was already in Malaya, as the Pioneers did not reach there until 1958. (Mike Keep collection)

Ex-RAF Provost XF682 in service with the air force of Muscat and Oman. (Mike Keep collection from an original by W.A. Harrison)

Another export Provost: SR136 in service with the air force of Southern Rhodesia. The flag over the door is a that of the Royal Air Force. (Mike Keep collection)

A Provost for the Irish Air Force, 190, at Luton. (PAC)

An armed Provost, UB201, for the Burmese Air Force. (PAC)

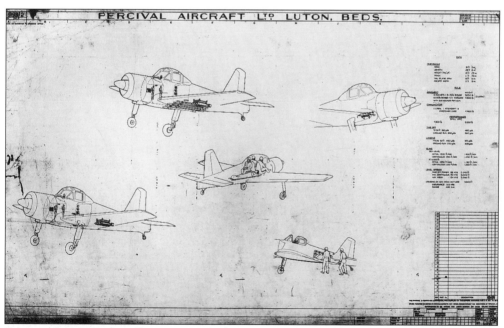

Schemes for various installations onto the basic Provost. Shown here are a stretcher installation and attendant for quick evacuations and two schemes for fitting up to twelve rockets and eight 20 lb bombs. These were given the Percivals' project number P.93.

Luton Airport in the late 1950s. The extension to the Percivals' assembly factory can be seen to the left, and the old farmhouse is still there at the top of the airport entrance driveway. The concrete runway has been laid and to the right are new, large hangars. In the lower right-hand corner the circular pit for the testing of helicopter blades is in the course of construction. The central grass area is now full of the International Airport buildings. (PAC)

# Four

# Name Changes

Although Percivals had firmly established itself as the leading post-war producer of training aircraft for the RAF, some forward-thinking people were convinced that training methods could be improved and in particular, the time involved in converting from piston-engined training aircraft into jet powered fighter aircraft.

An all-jet training programme was considered desirable by many. Consequently, design studies were begun by the company in 1953, under the direction of the new chief engineer, L.G. Frise. To speed up the design of the basic training aircraft many of the Provost components were taken as a basis. The result was the Jet Provost which had its initial flight at Luton on 26 June 1954. At this point all the piston Provost aircraft suddenly became known as Steam Provosts, after the prevalent comparisons of television and steam radio in the BBC comedy series *The Goon Show*!

After many service trials with a small batch of Jet Provost aircraft, in 1957 Percivals received large orders for the Jet Provost Mark 3 trainers, followed in later years by the improved Mark 4 versions. The initial Mark 3 aircraft did not enter service in the RAF until June 1959 but in 1954, as the company had changed its name to Hunting Percival Aircraft Ltd, all Jet Provosts were known as Hunting Percival Provosts. This continued until 1957, when the Percival name was dropped from the company titles. By this time Capt Edgar Percival had re-entered the aircraft manufacturing world in a separate company, so the changes were made to avoid confusion.

Shortly after L.G. Frise had joined the company, design work started on helicopters. The Ministry of Supply had, in 1951, initiated design work on rotor-tip powered machines and had placed an order with D. Napier and Sons for a small turbine gas-generator known as the Oryx. Napiers had had a large research establishment on the other side of the street from Percivals' since the middle of the war, and their experimental aircraft also flew from Luton airport. Consequently, in 1952, Hunting Percival Aircraft Ltd were awarded a contract to build a research helicopter to incorporate two Oryx engines. However, after many trials and tribulations, including many hours running trial rotors in a 'test pit', when the P.74 helicopter was ready to be tested for flight in May 1956, it declined to rise from the ground. There were many technical problems still to be solved when the contract was cancelled by the Ministry of Supply for political reasons.

Hunting Aircraft also looked into the possibility of building a short-haul jet-powered small airliner, the P.107, but its last aircraft design to be built was a Jet-Flap research aircraft. In 1956 Fred Pollicutt replaced L.G. Frise as technical director, and it was under his direction that the H.126 was designed and built. Only one aircraft was constructed and this had its first flight at the Royal Aircraft Establishment airfield at Bedford on 26 March 1963. Before this time however, and under severe political pressure from the government in power at the time to bring all the UK aircraft industry into two large organisations, Hunting Aircraft was amalgamated into the British Aircraft Corporation in September 1960. Manufacture of Jet Provosts continued at Luton for a short time afterwards, but the P.107 design was transferred to Weybridge in Surrey. The similar-looking BAC One-Eleven appeared in 1962.

On 8 December 1965 it was announced that BAC Luton would be closed in July 1966. Development and production of the BAC Jet Provost Mark 5 – the pressurised cockpit version – was transferred to Preston, Lancashire, and 1,850 employees at Luton were made redundant. W.A. (Bill) Summers retired as Assistant Managing Director of BAC (Operating) Ltd on 31 December 1966. The Jet Provost Mark 5 prototype flew on 28 February 1967 at Warton, Lancashire. The Luton factory was initially used by its neighbour Vauxhall Motors Ltd, but was soon afterwards completely demolished. The site was developed as a trading estate and today, only a few street names remain as echoes of the past.

A model of the P.74 research helicopter. This is as it was initially conceived, with a large fin, rudder and tailplane and without a tail rotor. (HPAL)

Another view of the P.74 model, showing the jet nozzles at the main rotor tips for the gas exhaust from the two Napier Oryx gas generators in the lower fuselage. The round exhaust on the lower side of the fuselage was a butterfly spill valve. (HPAL)

The prototype P.74 research helicopter, XK889, when built. The previous tail was replaced by a small rotor in the final design. The roll-out of the completed machine was in April 1956 and first-flight was attempted in May. However, it proved to be underpowered, the cyclic pitch system would not move and the machine would not leave the ground. It was eventually sold off for scrap after the government cut the funding. (HPAL)

A model of the P.84 Jet version of the Provost on the company stand at the 1952 Farnborough air display. (Norman H. Ellison)

The roll-out of the prototype Jet Provost, in June 1954, from the experimental department hangar. Note the tall undercarriage legs. (PAL)

The prototype Jet Provost Mk.1, XD674, ready for its first flight on 26 June 1954. The engine was an Armstrong-Siddeley Viper 101, giving a static thrust of 1,640 lbs. The unpainted aircraft shows the wing without the root extensions. (PAL PY4046)

The Jet Provost Mark 2 prototype, XD694, shows the much shorter undercarriage and the smoother fuselage lines compared to the Mark 1. (Armstrong-Siddeley XB68)

A flying view of the Mark 2 prototype, XD694, shows the original wings without the wing-tip tanks of the later versions. (Armstrong-Siddeley XB859)

A later photograph of the Mark 2 prototype Jet Provost, XD694, shows the instrument test boom fitted to the nose and the dorsal fin, which became common to all the later Jet Provost versions. The engine was now an Armstrong-Siddeley Viper 102 that produced a static thrust of 1,750 lbs. (HPAL)

The instrument panel of the Jet Provost Mark 3. Note the outlined basic flying instruments in the centre of the panel. (Mike Keep collection)

A standard production Jet Provost Mark 3, fitted with rockets, with the wing-tip tanks. In the cockpit two ejection seats were fitted. (HPAL)

The final assembly lines for the Jet Provost Mk.3 for the RAF, and the T.51 versions for export. The assembly lines are devoid of any Prince or Pembroke aircraft so the date must be about 1959 or 1960. (Mike Keep collection)

The reverse view of the previous photograph, showing the Jet Provosts in the same assembly line as the war-time Mosquitoes. The rounded windscreen was standard for the Mark 3 and Mark 4 versions. In the foreground is CJ704 for the Ceylon Air Force. (Mike Keep collection)

Jet Provost Mark 4, XP547. This was the last version built at Luton and had an Armstrong-Siddeley Viper 11 engine of 2,500 lb thrust. Deliveries to the RAF began in 1961, but they began to be phased out in 1968. (HPAL)

An armed Jet Provost T.Mk.52 '124' for Iraq. (HPAL)

A line-up of several Mark 52 Jet Provosts for Iraq. (HPAL PY9217)

One of fifteen Jet Provost T. Mk.52s exported to Venezuela, 'E040'. (HPAL)

A close up of the rocket and bombs fitted to the export versions of the Jet Provost. This installation was on the Ceylon Air Force T.51 aircraft. (HAL PY7511)

A model of the P.87 project. This was a 34- to 36-seat airliner, and the proposed engines may have been two Napier Nomads driving pusher propellers. (HPAL)

A model of the proposed 2-seat P.91 helicopter. This tip-powered machine may have been designed in 1954 to the Specification H.144T. Fairey Aviation Ltd built their Ultra-light helicopter, but no production contract was ever placed. (HPAL)

A development of the P.74 helicopter was proposed in 1955 as the P.105 ten-passenger commercial helicopter. The engine/rotor unit was a complete unit and could be fitted above any type of fuselage. The engines were Napier Oryx. (HPAL)

This model shows the lifting-crane version of the P.105, using the same engine/rotor unit as the ten-passenger version. (HPAL PY5378)

An artist's impression of the proposed H.107 airliner for 48 to 56 passengers. The two Bristol Orpheus B.Or.3 engines were rear-mounted. (HAL H10758)

A later impression of the H.107, but it now has a 'T' tail unit and fuselage painted up as British Aircraft Corporation 107. This version is very similar to the later BAC 1-11 airliner that was built at Weybridge. (HAL PY8512)

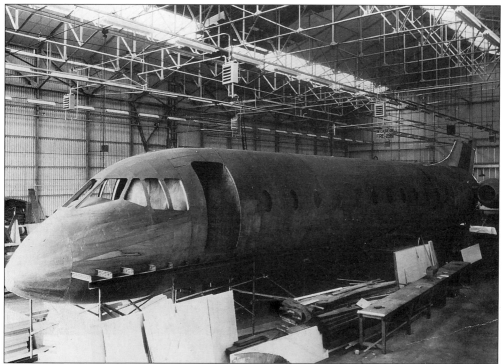

The wooden mock-up of the H.107 airline project. (HAL)

On the right is Pat Baker, who was chief draughtsman in the Design Office in the late nineteen-fifties, early sixties period. The others are family relatives, with Alison Hanton in the centre. (Alison Ellison, *née* Hanton)

The last type of aircraft designed and built at Luton was the H.126 jet-flap research aircraft, to investigate flight using the jet-flap principle of lift augmentation. Here the aircraft is shown being rolled out early in 1963. (Mike Keep collection)

The painted H.126 research aircraft, XN714, before its first flight. Note the patch of faded wartime camouflage still on the hangar roof above the fin. (HAL)

The H.126 being readied for its first flight. This took place at Turtle airfield, RAE Bedford on 26 March 1963. (Mike Keep collection)

The jet-flap in the down position along the wing. The engine was a single Bristol Siddeley Orpheus. (HAL)

The H.126 in flight. The thin chord of the wing is very noticeable in this view, contrasting with the fairly large fin and rudder. (HAL)

The H.126 landing at RAE Bedford. This aircraft is now preserved at the Royal Air Force Museum at Cosford. (HAL PY9960)

The later paint schemes adopted by the RAF for most of their training aircraft. This Mark 4 Jet Provost is at RAF Leeming in 1980. (Mike Keep collection)

For comparison, this is the Jet Provost Mark 5, with a pressurised cockpit and no wing-tip tanks. The Mark 5 versions were built by the British Aircraft Corporation at Warton, Lancashire, and the first flight was on 28 February 1967, after the Luton factory was closed. This Mark 5 was also at RAF Leeming in 1980. (Mike Keep collection)

The Hunting Harrier: a folding vehicle that could be carried in RAF communications aircraft such as the Pembroke. This first prototype was powered by a 650 cc BSA Type A.10 engine driving 16 inch diameter wheels. (HAL T4031)

The production batch of six Harrier vehicles for Army evaluation trials featured larger diameter wheels and could be driven through water 20 inches deep. The white overall suits were, hopefully, waterproof. (HAL PY7715)

# *Five*

# Postscript

Captain Percival was absent from the UK for much of the war, but he registered another company name on 18 July 1944. This was the E.W. Percival Aeronautical Co. at 72 Chesterfield House, Curson Street, London W1. Although he had resigned from the company at Luton in 1940, his contacts with it continued. David Luff, in his biography of Jim Mollison, relates that Jim negotiated the contract to deliver a Proctor 5 to Argentina by air with Percival himself, while in the bar of the Royal Aero Club, so the captain must have been acting as an agent for his old company around 1945.

Later travels around the world, including New Zealand in 1953, gave Percival ideas for the specification of an agricultural aircraft, the design for which began in 1954, when he established a small factory at Stapleford Tawney in Essex. The first flight of the E.P.9 aircraft was on 21 December 1955 by Percival, and the production of thirty-five aircraft was commenced. Sales were made to Australia, Germany, France, Libya and to British operators with contracts in Commonwealth countries. The new company was known by this time as Edgar Percival Aircraft Ltd, but the official change of name did not take place until 22 September 1959. However production had ceased in 1958, due to the ending of financial support after 'an interaction of vested interests.'

Percival sold the company to Samlesbury Engineering Ltd later in 1958, who then renamed it the Lancashire Aircraft Co. Ltd, and moved it to Samlesbury, Blackburn, Lancs. Included in the sale were seven unfinished airframes, all the jigs and tools, and two complete aircraft. The Earl of Bective was appointed sales manager with, in 1960, Geoff Sharples as chief designer. The new company was associated with Skyways and the British West Indian Airways during this period; the E.P.9 was then known as the Prospector. In 1962 it was decided to move the whole operation to Stansted Airport, but the company closed down later in the year after most of the company personnel declined to make the move to Essex. Plans for further aircraft, including the eight seater Prospector 4, came to nothing.

Percival meanwhile, continued aircraft design work at his London office.

Designs considered included supersonic aircraft, a 12-seat executive jet and other STOL aircraft. Sidney H. Parker was quoted as the company secretary in 1965, and was also listed as an engineer. Some of Percival's other interests during this period can be gained from the list of other companies of which he was a director, as quoted in company records: Associated British Engineering Ltd; Percival Power Units Ltd; Valbank Ltd; Valco Ltd and H. Widdip and Co. Ltd.

Captain Edgar Wickner Percival, C Eng, FRAeS, FIMechE, MSAE, MIAeE, AFIAeS, MIMarE, FRSA, died on 21 January 1984 at the age of 86.

A Prospector aircraft, powered by a 295 hp Lycoming engine. (Geoff Sharples)

An E.P.9 aircraft demonstrating the crop dusting qualities from the central fuselage hopper and the lower dump valve. (*Yorkshire Post*)

A Prospector aircraft, G-AOZO, landing at Samlesbury. The engine fitted to most E.P.9 and Prospector aircraft was a 295 hp Lycoming GO-480. (Geoff Sharples)

One of Lancashire's alterations from the E.P.9 design was the introduction of a set of windows in the lower hatch. This was introduced at the request of potential customers, so that they could study the correct distribution of the dust or spray or, as it was impolitely put, 'to watch the locusts get zapped.' (Geoff Sharples)

An alternative engine choice for the Prospector was a 370 hp Armstrong-Siddeley Cheetah 10, here seen fitted to the demonstrator G-ARDG. (Geoff Sharples)

# Six

# Social Times and Groups

In the days before television, evening entertainment usually meant reading or listening to the radio. Going out meant going down to the pub or to the club. Many wartime companies had highly organised sports and social clubs that catered for most people's spare time activities: cards, darts, snooker, football and rugby to name but a few. Most of these required celebrations at the well-stocked bar, either during the activity or afterwards, right up to the traditional time-honoured call of 'time gentlemen, please'. Percivals Aircraft's club house in Luton was in Castle Street. The site is now a car park where the inner ring-road cuts through to Stuart Street.

The sports and social club also organised most of the inter-office and inter-departmental sports championships, as well as the annual out door Field Day. This was a family affair, with competitive sports for all ages. Track and field events were surrounded by carnival booths, including Punch and Judy shows, rifle (.22) targets and sideshows. It was during the 1945 Field Day that the remains of Capt Percival's famous Mew Gull were burned. (See page 20) The sports and social club often also organised the annual Christmas dances, and the office dance was usually held at the George Hotel in George Street in the centre of Luton. This hotel was, for many years, the best hotel in Luton, and had the best ballroom floor until it was demolished and the site became part of the Arndale Centre. A later, favourite hotel was the Halfway House on Poynters Road, at the border between Luton and Dunstable.

The 1961/2 Design Office football team and coaches. From left to right, back row: Les Alcock, Ralph Fairbrother, -?-, David Waters, Syd Poynter, Ted Lenton, Erick Robinson, Les Edwards, Brian Kemp and Albert Thompson. Front row: Graham Biggs, George Mann, Bernard Childs (captain), Archie Warren and Tony Kraushaar. (HAL PY9206)

At a Halfway Hotel dance (the wallpaper confirms the place!) were, from left to right: -?-, Mrs Warren, Archie Warren, Rob Ridgwell and Alison Hanton. (Parrott Studios Ltd)

Mr Thompson and Alison Hanton in full flight, at the Halfway House. (Parrott Studios Ltd)

Table No. 2 at the Christmas dance at the George, in 1961. From left to right: Jacqueline Everard, Sybil Parrish, -?-, Julie Ridewood, John Ridewood, Harold Parrish, -?-, and Mrs ? Champken. (HAL PY8201)

The ad hoc amateur concert party: an essential ritual that had to be endured at each office dance or function. From left to right: Roy Champken, Bernie Childs, Ted Lenton, Rob Ridgwell, -?-, Eric Robinson and -?-. (Parrott Studios Ltd)

The typical office going-away official presentation of gifts, group photograph, so beloved of company photographers who would use any excuse to order their colleagues around. This group was from the Weights Office in 1961 and Mr Henderson, head of the Weights Group, is making the presentation. (HAL PY9018)

On the left is Ian Parker, head of the Statistics Group within the Design Office, with Len ? from the Weights Group. (Alison Hanton)

The Hunting Aircraft Ltd Stress Office group in 1961. From left to right, back row: Harold King, Bob Sellars, Frank Nichols, Derek Samson, Harrold Parrish, Peter Eberhard, Jeff Hearn, Harry Ward, Malcolm Wright, John Lay and Mr Green. Front row: Neddy ? , John Ridewood, -?-, -?-, Ron Barton, -?-, and Mr Thompson. (HAL PY8225)

Frank Nichols and John Lay were fellow apprentices of the author. Most of these names have been recalled from the memories of the ex-Percival and Hunting employees now here in Seattle. We apologise if our memories have misplaced or forgotten some of the names.

# Seven

# My Time at Percivals

As a schoolboy living in Luton throughout the Second World War, much spare time was spent leaning over the airport security fence looking at the aircraft, especially at the experimental aircraft based at D. Napier and Sons' part of the airport. The special versions of the Hawker Tempest were always of interest, but my favourite was the Blackburn Firebrand Mark 1, an aircraft of elegant lines.

When the time came to leave school in 1947, having been an active member of the National Association of Spotters Clubs at the Luton Grammar School throughout the war, an aviation career seemed not only natural but anything else was hardly worth considering. As we were members of an aviation club, we had been allowed to visit the Percivals' factory several times just after the war ended. During our first visit we were shown the complete production sequences of the Mosquito manufacture and also, the first Proctor 5 aircraft being prepared for the post-war civil market. One of these was the special Proctor being prepared for Jim Mollison to fly to Argentina, so the date of our visit must have been either December 1945 or January 1946. Consequently, to a sixteen year old aircraft-mad kid, there was no other place even to consider seeking employment than at Percival Aircraft Ltd at Luton.

I started there in September 1947 as an office junior and later joined the apprenticeship course in April 1948. For the next three years I worked in many of the production departments, including the machine shop, tool room, sheet metal, fuselage assembly, wings and final assembly shops including the experimental department. For the last two years it was the planning department followed by the jig and tool design office. This I enjoyed the most; consequently, I graduated from the apprenticeship as a fully qualified jig and tool designer. There followed two years National Service in the Fleet Air Arm of the Royal Navy, during which, as a part of training to become an aircrew observer, I flew in the Sea Princes that I had been working on at Percivals for the last few years.

Later aircraft employment was with Auster Aircraft Ltd, Rearsby, Leicester; Armstrong-Whitworth Aircraft Ltd at Baginton, Coventry, and Slingsby

Sailplanes Ltd of Kirbymoorside, Yorkshire. Finally it was with various divisions of the Boeing Commercial Airplane Co. Ltd in the Seattle area, from which I retired on 1 July 1995, still an aircraft-mad kid.

The 1949 group of Percivals Aircraft apprentices. In the front centre is George Archer, the apprentice supervisor and, on his left, Jack Caswell, who was in charge of the apprentice workshop and training room. The author is at the top left. (PAL PY2296)

The annual prize-winning apprentices for 1949. The author is on the left, and Peter Trotman is second from the right. (PAL PY1795)

The author's turn to have the popular apprentice photographic flight. The aircraft was Prentice VR321, with Dick Wheldon as pilot, the author in the right seat and Brian Clarke in the rear. The flight was from Luton Airport on 7 April 1949. (PAL, taken from Proctor 5 G-AGTC)

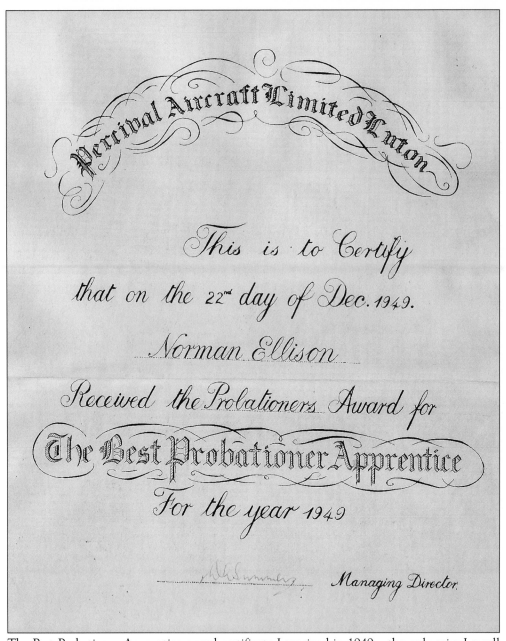

**Percival Aircraft Limited Luton**

This is to Certify

that on the 22ⁿᵈ day of Dec. 1949.

*Norman Ellison*

Received the Probationers Award for

**The Best Probationer Apprentice**

For the year 1949

_____ Managing Director

The Best Probationer Apprentice award certificate I received in 1949 – the only prize I recall receiving at Percivals. It was signed by W.A. Summers as managing director.

# *Eight*
# Shadows of the Past

This book is being compiled in 1997 and it is, therefore, sixty-five years since the first classic Gulls began to appear. Consequently it is not surprising that there are now very few of the early Percivals' aeroplanes still to be seen in flying condition. However, there are some still to be seen in museums around the world and this is a representative list of some of these.

Gull 4, G-ACGR, in the Brussels Air Museum, Belgium.
Gull 6, G-ADPR, on display at Auckland International Airport, New Zealand.
Mew Gull, G-AEXF, under restoration at the Shuttleworth Trust, Old Warden, Bedfordshire.
Q-6, one is believed to be under restoration in the Isle of Man.
Proctor 3, LZ766, Imperial War Museum, Duxford, Cambridgeshire.
Proctor 4, NP294, Lincolnshire Aviation Heritage Centre, East Kirkby, Lincolnshire.
Prentice, VR259, Air Atlantique Historic Flight, Coventry Airport, Warwickshire.
Prince, G-AMLZ, under restoration at Caernarfon Air Museum, Gwynedd, Wales.
Sea Prince T. Mk.1, WF122, Cornwall Aero Park, Culdrose Manor, Helston, Cornwall.
Pembroke, WV746, at the Aerospace Museum, Cosford, Shropshire.
Provost T. Mk.1, WV605, Norfolk and Suffolk Aviation Museum, Flixton, Suffolk.
Jet Provost T. 1, G-AOBU, under restoration at Cranfield, Bedfordshire.
Jet Provost T. 3A, XM383, Newark Air Museum, Winthorpe, Newark, Nottinghamshire.
Jet Provost T. 5A, XW323. at The Royal Air Force Museum, Hendon, London.
Hunting H.126, XN714, The Aerospace Museum, Cosford, Shifnal, Shropshire.

Proctor 3, LZ766, at the Imperial War Museum, Duxford, Cambridge, in May 1996. Sold as surplus in May 1949, it was registered G-ALCK until June 1963 when it was withdrawn from use at Woolsington. It was donated to the Skyfame Museum at Staverton and, when that closed, it was sent to Duxford and restored. (Norman H. Ellison)

Prentice T.Mk.1 VR192 at the Second World War Aircraft Preservation Society, Lasham airfield, Alton, Hants in 1995. One of the pre-production batch, it was sold as surplus out of the RAF in 1957 to Aviation Traders, Southend. Registered G-APIT, it was civilianised and sold by them to Airwork Ltd, Perth, on 10 August 1958. It was later used by Scottish Gas Ltd, Perth, and then transferred to CAVU International at Jersey, until it was withdrawn from use in October 1970. It is now under restoration. (Norman H. Ellison)

Sea Prince C. Mk.1 WF137, at Lasham, with Prentice VR192 in 1995. This is the same aircraft as the Sea Prince on page 74. It did not appear to be under restoration, or very well protected when the author visited the museum; there were not even any control locks on any of the flying control surfaces. (Norman H. Ellison)

Provost T. Mk.1 WV562, at the Aerospace Museum, RAF Cosford, Shropshire, in 1995. There are many Provosts still flying privately. (Bob Ridgwell)

Pembroke C.1 WV753 at the former Wales Museum, now closed. It was last used by the RAF Training Command and may not now exist. (Mike Eacock)

There is a fine collection of aircraft engines in the aviation wing of the Science Museum, South Kensington, London. On one of the racks in November 1995, was this example of the Napier Oryx gas producer engine of 750 gas hp. Above the engine is mounted one of the jet nozzles that could have been used on the P.74 helicopter. (Norman H. Ellison)

# Bibliography

As this book concentrates on the aircraft built by Percival Aircraft Ltd, no attempt has been made to relate the many exploits by the famous people that flew them all round the world. For further reading and study, here is an abbreviated listing of books about the famous pilots and others.

Babington Smith, Constance, *Amy Johnson*, (Patrick Stephens 1988)
Batten, Jean, *Alone in the Sky*, (reprinted by Airlife Publishing Co., 1979)
Boughton, Terence, *The Story of the British Light Aeroplane*, (John Murray, 1963)
Cadogan, Mary, *Woman with Wings*, (Academy Chicago Publishers, 1992)
Davis, Pedr, *Charles Kingsford Smith*, (Marque Publishing Co. Pty. Ltd, 1988)
Jackson, A.J., *British Civil Aircraft* Volumes 1 and 2, (Putnam and Co., London, 1960) and
    Volume 3 of the revised second edition.
Lovell, Mary S., *Straight on till Morning; the Biography of Beryl Markham*, (Hutchinson
    Ltd, London,1987)
Luff, David, *Mollison, The Flying Scotsman*, (Lidun Publishing, 1993)
Mackersey, Ian, *Jean Batten, The Garbo of the Skies*, (Macdonald and Co., 1990)
Markham, Beryl, *West with the Night*, (reprinted by North Point Press, 1987)
Silvester, John, *Percival and Hunting Aircraft*, (John Silvester, 1987)
Trzebinski, Errol, *The Lives of Beryl Markham*, (William Heinemann Ltd, 1993)
Wixey, Kenneth, *Parnall Aircraft since 1914*, (Putnam Aeronautical Books, 1990)

# Acknowledgements

This book is, of necessity, a compilation of the facts, figures and writings of others, and it is hoped that acknowledgement has been quoted where due. The origin of the photographs included here has been quoted where known. However, the original starting point of my collection was a large parcel of photographs donated to me in January 1966 by employees who were about to lose their employment when the Luton factory closed down. Most of these photographs are believed to have been Percivals Aircraft copyright, but this cannot be proven. Neither can it be determined now, whether they were photographs that required permission to be published, or whether they were free issue from the company.

Many photographs have been loaned to me by Mike Eacock of Sherborne, Dorset, who was at Percivals at Luton from 1944 onwards for many years. His assistance has been invaluable, especially in his ability to extract the many photographs that originated from the collection and records kept by the late Mike Keep.

I would like to express my gratitude to the following people in England for assistance in obtaining photographs for this book: Mr Richard Riding (editor of *Aeroplane Monthly*); Mr A.W.L. Nayler (Technical Manager of The Royal Aeronautical Society); Mr Alex Henshaw; Alison Hodge (publisher); Elizabeth Adey (Keeper of Local History, Luton Museum Service); Luton Library; Ms Christine Gregory (Reprographic Services Officer, Royal Air Force Museum, Hendon); Jane Gowman, (Photo Library, Associated Press, London) and Laurence Pollinger Ltd (authors' agents, London). Also to John Silvester, Luton; Richard Macdemitria, Crawley; my brother Robert John Ellison in Woking and my nephew Adam Ellison in Luton, for following up on leads and information that I did not have time to check upon during my short visits to England.

For photographs and information: Randy Acord (Curator of the Alaskaland Pioneer Air Museum); Alistair Kennedy (Marque Publishing Co., Hurstville, NSW); Andrew Foulds (Manager, Fairfax Photo Library, Sydney); Lily Oei (Watkins/Loomis Agency, New York) and Harry Koundakjian, (Photo Library, Associated Press, New York).

Finally, to friends and ex-Percivals, Hunting Percival and Hunting Aircraft employees who now live in the Seattle area, Mr Harry Ward, Mr John Ridewood, Mr Bob Ridgwell and their wives. Also my wife Alison (*née* Hanton), who has been my helpful critic throughout this project, and to Mr Geoff Sharples, ex-Lancashire Aircraft Ltd, another member of our circle of British friends here in America.

I am indebted to Mr Alan Sutton and to Mr David Buxton of the Chalford Publishing Company, for their help during the creation of this book.

Norman H. Ellison
Bellevue, Seattle. USA
1997